IMAGES
of America

AROUND GREAT
BARRINGTON AND
STOCKBRIDGE

The "Old Man of Monument Mountain" is distantly related to his stone-faced namesake in New Hampshire. Although conceived in different bedrock, both landmarks were raised by Mother Nature. While gazing at this profile, consider the following quote attributed to Daniel Webster (revised to be politically and geographically correct): "People hang out signs indicative of their respective trades. The shoemaker hangs out a gigantic shoe; a jeweler displays a monstrous watch; even the dentist hangs out a gold tooth. But up on Monument Mountain, God Almighty has hung out a sign to show that (s)he creates people!" (Arthur Palme photograph courtesy of Stockbridge Library Association.)

IMAGES
of America

AROUND GREAT BARRINGTON AND STOCKBRIDGE

Gary T. Leveille

ARCADIA

Published by Arcadia Publishing,
an imprint of the Chalford Publishing Corporation,
One Washington Center, Dover, New Hampshire 03820.
Printed in Great Britain

Library of Congress Cataloging-in-Publication Data applied for

Dedicated to Verna Houff
who understands

Special thanks to Bernie Drew, Bob Jones, Jim Parrish, and Polly Pierce
for their incredible help and support

Audrey, Justin, and Katelyn Leveille
for their patience

In memory of Alec and Thelma Ochs
who pointed the way

For their support and encouragement, thanks to Les Beebe, Amy Giroux, Anne Grosser, Tully Hall, Randi Toder Haskins, Charles Houff, Neuza Langhans, Pamela Faith Lerman, and Joy Milani-Lane. For inspiration, thanks to Alison Shaw. For being such talented colleagues and nice neighbors, thanks to Donna Christian, Elizabeth Mackney, Allison McMillan-Lee, Margaret Perry Shea, and Chris Schubach.

On a chilly day in the 1930s, eager skiers line up in front of Heaton Hall in Stockbridge. (David Milton Jones photograph courtesy of Stockbridge Library Association.)

Contents

Acknowledgments   6

Introduction   7

1.   All for Fun, and Fun for All   9

2.   You Can't Get There From Here   25

3.   You Can Always Go Downtown   43

4.   It's a Tough Job, but Somebody's Got to Do It   57

5.   There's No Place Like Home   71

6.   Hands to Work, Hearts to God   85

7.   Beauty or the Beast   103

8.   Family, Friends, and Neighbors   117

Acknowledgments

Creating this book has been an incredible experience. I've had the opportunity to meet many wonderful people and renew old friendships. Residents throughout Berkshire County have welcomed me into their homes to share special memories. I have looked at thousands of photographs, each with a special story to tell.

Pretend for a moment that you and your family are shipwrecked on an island. Now imagine how you'd feel if the captain of the rescue boat told you to leave some family members behind because the boat was too small to hold everyone. That's the frustration I felt trying to whittle down nearly 600 of my favorite photographs to 237. It was, at times, agonizing. These photographs had become a part of my family. I lived with them for many months. They took over my office as well as my son's room. But, finally, the job was done. So when this book sells well and the publisher asks me to do a second one, I'll be able to "rescue" the rest of the photographs to share with you!

My heartfelt appreciation to the brilliant photographers, past and present, whose wonderful works grace these pages. Unlike many books which list photograph credits in tiny type on a back page, this one includes credit where credit is due—with each photograph. (There are some instances where the photographer is unknown.)

Thanks to the many family, friends, neighbors, businesses, and organizations for their help: Elinore Agar; Lucien Aigner; Barbara Allen and Patrick Flynn of the Berkshire County Historical Society; Diane and Steve Arnold; Buddy and Doreen Atwood; Sharon Bailey of the Ramsdell Library; David Barnum; Frank and Jinny Beattie; *The Berkshire Eagle*; Betros Market; Jean Blackmur; Danae Boissevain and Bernard Rogers of Simon's Rock College; David and Anne Braman; Grace Brown; Claudette Callahan of the New Marlborough Historical Society; Tony Carlotto and Steve Carlotta of the Snap Shop; John Conway; Helen Carroll; Ann Carroll Klein; Jamie Carter; Jack and Betsy Cook; Jane Anderson Costa; Froni Crane; Jack Dezieck; Bernie and Donna Drew; Marlene Drew and Peggy Sullivan of the Mason Public Library; Olga Dunn; April Ehrenman; Edward Ely; Ely's Market; Mike Fitzpatrick and Great Barrington's Hope Fire Company; Rachel Fletcher; Reverend Joseph Forte; Rosemary Gibbons; Irma Giegold; Kinsley Goodrich; Donald Graham; Kelly Gray; Charles Gunn; Larry and Linda Hankey; Richard Hankey; Nancy MacDonald Hecker of Apple Hill Design; Claire and Gordon Height; Kim Hines of Gould Farm; Marge Horelly; Betsy Holtzinger of the Gingham Rabbit; Barrie Hughes; John B. Hull III; Bob Jones and Pat Mullin Jones of the Great Barrington Historical Society; Clemens Kalischer; Joe Kellogg; Jim Kotleski; Walt Koladza of Berkshire Aviation Enterprises; Louie Lamone; Al Lenardson; Joy Milani-Lane and Greg Lane; David Lane; Paul and Marie Laramee; Sandy and Paul Larkin; Robert Lohbauer; Art Marasco; Ted Mohr; Laurie McLeod; John and Eileen Mooney; Monterey Historical Society; Don and Priscilla Moulthrop; Richard Nault; John Nichols; Arlene Norton of the Red Lion Inn; James Parrish and Lila Parrish of the Great Barrington Historical Commission; Jim Peace; Louis Peyron and Francis Pilling of the Stockbridge Fire Department; Polly Pierce and Cathy Buffoni of the Stockbridge Library Association; Frank Ptak of the Fred Sauer Photo Archives; James Saunders; Dick Snow; Irene Tague; Joan Roger and Tom Jaworski of WSBS Radio; Cris Raymond of the Stockbridge Bowl Association; Judy Rupinski; David Rutstein; Sanjiban Sellew; Barbara Shiminsky; Linda Szekely of the Norman Rockwell Museum; Walter H. Scott; David Wade Smith; Lindy Smith; Wanda Styka and Paul Ivory of Chesterwood Museum; John Tracy of Gorham & Norton's Market; Reverend Charles Van Ausdall; Donald Victor; William Walsh of the Great Barrington Police Department; Ann Walsh; Julie Westervelt of Kripalu Center; Richard Wilcox of the Stockbridge Police Department; Roberta Wheeler; Ruth Wolfsdorf; Artis Wood of Berkshire Botanical Garden; Helen and Sonny Zanetti; Rabbi Deborah Zecher; and Edgar Zukauskas.

Introduction

Southern Berkshire County is a magical place. Some call it paradise. Stockbridge summer resident and famed sculptor David Chester French once said to a New York reporter, "I spend six months of the year up there, it is heaven."

Those of us who live here or visit regularly know of the special synergy that exists between "The Arts" of human creation and those presented by Mother Nature. Consider the splendid sculpture of Mr. French alongside the glacial carvings atop Monument Mountain. Feel the soothing breeze on Lake Mahkeenac as the music of Aaron Copeland's "Appalachian Spring" soars from Tanglewood's shed.

Experience the magnificence of Searles Castle as it towers over the meandering Housatonic River. Discover the nostalgic artistry of Norman Rockwell near the edge of a wildflower meadow. Whether dance or theater, forest or waterfall, we are surrounded by the best of both worlds. No wonder so many who reside here suspect South County is the center of the universe!

The Berkshires were first inhabited by Mahican Native Americans, part of the Algonquin nation. Evidence indicates that there was a substantial Native American population in the area of present-day Great Barrington hundreds, if not thousands, of years before the arrival of Europeans. By the time the Dutch and English arrived in 1730, the Mahicans were living in two small villages, one at Stockbridge and one in Sheffield. According to tradition, the Mahican Indian population had been in steady decline during the one hundred and fifty years preceding the establishment of Stockbridge. The tribe had been reduced in size by war with the Mohawk Indians and driven from the Hudson Valley back to their ancestral hunting grounds along the Housatonic. In 1736, a permanent Indian mission was established in Stockbridge and the remaining Indian population moved there. Before long, the Stockbridge Indians were coerced into leaving their home and moving West. Although most of the early white settlers in South County were of English extraction (from Connecticut, Rhode Island, and eastern Massachusetts), many Dutch families also came here from adjacent areas of New York.

Until the 1820s, Great Barrington and Stockbridge remained essentially rural, farming communities. By the time the railroad arrived in 1842, business was booming! Over one hundred years ago, Irish, Polish, and Italian immigrants came to work in the factories and on the railroads. The rich and famous came to build their vacation "cottages." Whether tycoon or tailor, laborer or lawyer, factory worker or farmer, all called these hills home. And all the while, the tourists came. They still do. Over the years, many former visitors have adopted the Berkshires as their new home.

Much has changed here in South County over the past one hundred and twenty-five years— the period covered photographically in this book. Once-thriving textile factories have been replaced by hi-tech, special effects companies. Once-bustling boomtowns have grown quieter, but still nurture a menagerie of cottage industries and historic homes. Turn-of-the-century technical advances by inventors like William Stanley have been replaced by the entrepreneurial inventiveness of businesspersons like Jane Fitzpatrick. Where Monument Mills bedspreads once lay, Country Curtains ® now hang.

The photographs in this book are primarily from the towns of Great Barrington and Stockbridge, including the villages of Housatonic, Van Deusenville, Glendale, and Interlaken. Views of Egremont, Lenox, Monterey, New Marlborough, Sheffield, and South Lee are also included. These images offer a rare glimpse through the window to our past. Each photograph is a reflection of the people and places that existed where we now live. Who were these people? What can we learn from them?

These images have been gathered from a variety of collections, both private and public. In addition to the rare nineteenth- and early-twentieth-century images, many superb photographs from the last fifty years are also included. By looking at the whole picture, the connections between our distant and recent past will become more apparent. By understanding where we've been, we'll have a better idea of where we're at, and where we're headed. So, welcome to Great Barrington and Stockbridge, *then and now*. Enjoy!

Gary T. Leveille

Since 1895, this bronze-skinned waif, tarnished by the tears of time, has watched life pass by in the fast lane of Route 23 in Great Barrington. The Newsboy fountain was given to the town by William Lee Brown, teacher, miner, politician, entrepreneur, and part-owner of the first *New York Daily News*. In honor of the Newsboy's one-hundredth "birthday," the ailing statue was restored by the New England Association of Circulation Executives (a newspaper trade group) in association with the Great Barrington Historical Society. (Courtesy of Leveille Collection.)

One
All for Fun,
and Fun for All

Talented townsfolk in Great Barrington gather at the Mahaiwe Theater to promote *The Country Fair*, a stage play produced to benefit the Visiting Nurse Association, *c*. 1910. After the Mahaiwe opened in 1905, many famous personalities of that era graced the local stage, including John Philip Sousa, Eddie Foy, Ed Wynn, and DeWolf Hopper (*Casey at the Bat*). In addition to live shows, the theater began showing movies. The blinking, multi-bulb marquee that now hangs at the entranceway was not added until the 1930s. (A.M. Costello photograph courtesy of Great Barrington Historical Society.)

Hats off to these cleverly coiffured young ladies. This hat contest was one of several entertaining events sponsored by the Laurel Festival in the early 1970s. Does anybody know which hat won? From left to right are Mary Delmolino, Lynn Davis, Penny Call, Diane Moulthrop, Sherry Candee, and Diane Clark. (Courtesy of the Moulthrop family.)

There's no skirting this issue, laddy. A wee bit of Scotland and a few familiar faces are found in this festive scene. From left to right are Senator Jack Fitzpatrick, Ruth Downs, Hugh Downs, Jane Fitzpatrick, Anne Auchincloss, and Gordon Auchincloss. (Art Marasco photograph courtesy of Stockbridge Library Association.)

10

With the exception of the round Shaker barn in Pittsfield, Egremont's Jug End barn was probably the most famous in Berkshire County. Jug End resort was created in 1935 when an entrepreneur, Major Hugh Smiley, converted his ultra-modern dairy barn into an all-season vacation site. Herds of tourists stampeded to the popular barnyard. Jug End achieved its greatest fame with owners (and marketing geniuses) Angus and Mimi MacDonald. Images of the famous barn appeared on television, in magazines, even on record albums! At the height of the 1980s' real estate boom, Jug End resort was sold. A large housing development was planned, but fell through. The state finally acquired the property and tore down most of the buildings. Today the land is used for hiking and cross-country skiing. (Courtesy of Nancy MacDonald Hecker.)

Here's Johnny! Mimi and Angus MacDonald of Jug End resort meet with Johnny Carson in the mid-1950s. Mimi once appeared on Carson's TV game show, "Who Do You Trust?" (Courtesy of Nancy MacDonald Hecker.)

To paraphrase Henry David Thoreau, "A lake is Mother Earth's most expressive feature. It is Earth's eye, upon looking into which, you may measure the depth of your own nature." Overlooking Stockbridge Bowl (Lake Mahkeenac), these hikers are in search of the perfect picnic spot. Hope somebody told them about the poison ivy! This 1950s view was snapped near the Seranak estate owned by Tanglewood. (Clemens Kalischer photograph.)

Skating on Stockbridge Bowl has always been a popular pastime, especially in the winter! Around the turn of the century, Katherine Story (in the foreground) and Caroline Stokes (at left) slice the ice in front of the Shadowbrook boathouse. (Courtesy of Berkshire County Historical Society.)

Josephine Choate, daughter of famed attorney and ambassador Joseph Choate, enjoys swimming with her puppy at Stockbridge Bowl c. 1890. Josephine died in 1896, while only in her twenties. Her well-known sister, Mabel Choate, lived at the Naumkeag estate in Stockbridge and is featured elsewhere in this book. (Courtesy of the Naumkeag Collection, The Trustee of Reservations.)

Here's the Mahkeenac Boat Club on Stockbridge Bowl in the early 1900s. The building still stands and the boat club remains a social and sailing mecca on the lake. (Courtesy of Leveille Collection.)

Introducing the Searles High School Women's Basketball Team for 1944. From left to right are (front row) Frances Moskowitz, Dot Casey, and Phyllis House; (back row) Ann Tripodes, Josephine Joseph, Martha White, Claire Kellogg, Carol Hinds, and Jeanne Adams. (Courtesy of double-dribbler Claire Kellogg Height.)

Great Barrington's Hope Fire Company softball team knows how to swing a bat and handle a hose! Team records have been lost, however, possibly on purpose. From left to right in this c. 1942 photograph are (sitting in front) Charles Condon, Sid Shultis, and Abe Hammer; (second row) Bill Welch, Arch Lamont, Harold Atwood, Joe Maley, Charles Benham, Ed McCormick, Gus Tries, and George Atwood; (leaning on the truck) Art Cunningham and Gordon Hammer. (Courtesy of Hope Fire Company.)

Back in the late 1930s, a group of Great Barrington hockey enthusiasts formed a team sponsored by the Cove Inn on Stockbridge Road. Their rink was located where the Cove Bowling Lanes are now. Here is the 1941 team. From left to right are (front row) Ricco Zucco, Dave McGraw, Tom Busby, Bob Kinne, and George Bower; (back row) Lou Storti, Jack Hawley, Fred Gifford, Roy Kinne, Les Allen, and Ray Gifford. (Nault photograph courtesy of Great Barrington Historical Society.)

As the scoreboard in the background indicates, the Stockbridge Baseball Club is waiting to take on the Rising Paper team. (David Milton Jones photograph courtesy of Stockbridge Library Association.)

"And that's the way it is at Butternut Basin in the 1960s. This is Walter Cronkite reporting." (Marie Tassone photograph courtesy of Great Barrington Historical Society.)

If that girl jumps off a building, does that mean you should? Only if you have a Great Barrington guardian snow angel like this one! This flaky free-fall took place in the mid-1970s. (Steven Arnold photograph.)

The king of this Searles High School prom is Dick Snow, now the retired king of Wheeler & Taylor Insurance in Great Barrington. The queen is Christina Nowakowski. The year is 1960 and the royal court includes, from left to right, Jane Gilligan, Janet Robinson, Jean Oggiani, unknown, Marie Cochran, and Barbara Wetmore. (Marie Tassone photograph courtesy of Great Barrington Historical Society.)

The Great Barrington Bridge Club was formed in 1936 and is still going strong sixty years later! Shown here about 1960, from left to right, are Iva Albano, Bobbie O'Keefe, Rose Gardella, Elinore Agar, Lila Parrish, Gertrude Snyder, Ruth Beers, and Gladys Osgood. Guess which one has the marked cards! (Robert Parrish photograph courtesy of Elinore Agar.)

In the 1870s, John Van Bramer purchased property in North Egremont surrounding Prospect Lake. On the east shore he built the Cliff House shown in this 1880s photograph. The building and picnic area were later purchased and improved by William and Florence Siter. In 1958, Bill and Helen Carroll bought the park and developed it into a popular campground. Today, it is the oldest surviving, privately-owned campground in the Berkshires. (J. Hall photograph courtesy of Leveille Collection.)

This towering water slide was built by William Carroll to replace a smaller dockside slide that existed for many years at Prospect Lake. This view was taken about 1965. (Courtesy of Leveille Collection.)

A captivated crowd gathers at the Great Barrington Town Hall on July 4, 1894, to hear the Silver Coronet Marching Band. (Courtesy of Great Barrington Historical Commission.)

World-renowned artist and Stockbridge resident Norman Rockwell studies an edible work of art offered in celebration of his eighty-second birthday in 1976. The kids hope their hometown hero will "let them eat cake!" (Eileen Mooney photograph.)

This early 1900s Stockbridge sewing circle sits on the porch of Mrs. Daniel Williams' home on Main Street (later the Rose Coffee House, now the yellow residence across the street from the library). The group includes several familiar Stockbridge residents such as Suzanne Perry, Marion Bidwell, Helen Bidwell, Mrs. Williams (with nurse), Rachel Field, Karl Bidwell, and Elizabeth Field. (Courtesy of Stockbridge Library Association.)

The sidewalk on Main Street in Stockbridge was once a quieter, gentler place. Here, in front of St. Paul's Episcopal Church (next to Clark's Drug Store), several young lads watch attentively as three adults play marbles! Hope they are playing for "funzies" and not "keepzies." (Courtesy of Stockbridge Library Association.)

The Gibson's Grove steamer at Lake Buel was a catamaran paddle-wheeler built during our nation's centennial. A wood-fired steam boiler propelled the boat along at a poky 5 mph. The boat operated for ten years until it caught fire and burned up. (J. Hall photograph courtesy of Mason Public Library.)

Who needs Florida when locals had their own Miami Beach on the Monterey side of Lake Buel? This popular picnic area was one of several on the lake. (Courtesy of Leveille Collection.)

Soaking up the sun at Teggi's Miami Beach on Lake Buel, from left to right, are (front row) Nancy Stewart, Sis Zanetti, ? Spadaccini, and Dorothy Jamison; (back row) Ed Supernaugh, Richard Nault, Richard Renzel, Robert Smith, Jim Stewart, and Jack Smith. (Nault photograph.)

In 1949, this seaplane from Island Airways Flying School (NYC) dropped in for a visit at Lake Buel. On the dock, from left to right, are Quint and Jo Zanetti, Teena Zanetti, Mrs. Tuller, A.P. Culver, Mr. Tuller, and Leo Wells. (Courtesy of Zanetti Collection.)

Did you see what I saw? Rachel Sisson, Eleanor Sisson, and Helen Sheldon enjoy the ups and downs of summertime fun in early 1900s New Marlborough. (Sisson photograph courtesy of New Marlborough Historical Society.)

The Housatonic Agricultural Society Exhibition, later known as the Great Barrington Fair, began in a vacant lot off Main Street in 1842. Twelve years later, the society purchased the South Main Street property where the fairground remains today. In its hay-filled heyday, the fair was a social highlight of the year. But as agriculture's role in the Berkshire economy diminished, the fair became an aging dinosaur, struggling to survive. In 1995, a tornado tore through the fairground. WSBS radio newsman Tom Jaworski reported moments later, "The fairground is no more. It's gone." Today, fair enthusiasts are rebuilding the site. (Courtesy of Leveille Collection.)

You can almost hear the horses gallop by in this 1940s view of the Great Barrington Fair. (Ted Webster photograph courtesy of Edna Webster Foster.)

The Great Barrington Fair midway has always been a favorite of youngsters. Photographer Al Lenardson captured the beauty and excitement of the Ferris wheel and other rides in this dazzling photograph. (Courtesy of Ice House Studio.)

An early zeppelin prototype is launched at the Great Barrington Fair in the early 1900s. Commenting about the bizarre balloon, local historian Roz LaFontana said, "It looked like a mole going both ways." (Courtesy of Leveille Collection.)

Two

You Can't Get There From Here

The next time you're sitting in summertime traffic on Stockbridge Road in Great Barrington, think of this photograph! You're looking north toward Monument Mountain, c. 1902. Note the trolley tracks on the right. But where is McDonald's? (R.L. Burghardt photograph courtesy of Great Barrington Historical Society.)

Berkshire Street Railway trolleys navigate a sea of spectators on Main Street during Great Barrington's 150th anniversary in 1911. Town hall is decorated with banners, as is the Mahaiwe Block on Main Street. Note the location of the original bandstand in front of the town hall. (A.M. Costello photograph courtesy of Great Barrington Historical Commission.)

An open-car trolley rolls down Main Street in Glendale, c. 1920s. (Courtesy of Stockbridge Library Association.)

Here's the Stockbridge trolley station as it appeared in 1914. Maintained by the Berkshire Street Railway, it was located west of the train station on the other side of Route 7. (Berkshire Valuation photograph courtesy of Kinsley Goodrich Collection.)

Another trolley waiting station still stands on the corner of Route 7 and Park Street in Stockbridge. It is now used for storage by the parks and recreation department. (Courtesy of Kinsley Goodrich Collection.)

It looks mighty busy at the Stockbridge railroad station in this 1950s photograph. (Clemens Kalischer photograph.)

All is quiet in the roomy interior of the Great Barrington railroad station c. 1954. Note the chalkboard train schedule. When the depot was built in 1901, the tracks were raised, Castle Street was cut off, and a pedestrian subway tunnel was built under the tracks. The station is now a restaurant. (Charles Gunn photograph.)

In 1911, two freight trains collided near the North Plain Road underpass in Great Barrington. A crowd quickly gathered and deemed the event a smashing success. (Photograph courtesy of Jim Peace.)

The tiny hamlet of Van Deusenville once supported two textile mills, a rope factory, an iron ore blast furnace, a saw mill, a chair manufacturer, a wagon maker, a post office, a tavern, a church, three stores, and a sizable train station. In fact, by the 1840s, the prosperous village was competing with Great Barrington to open the first bank. (Barrington won.) The train depot was torn down in 1940, leaving an empty lot next to the former Trinity Episcopal Church (site of the 1969 movie *Alice's Restaurant*). (Courtesy of Charles Gunn and the Dave Peters Collection.)

This classic car and its owner are getting cranked up at MacClintic's Garage (now a convenience store) on the corner of Park Street and Route 7 in Stockbridge. (David Milton Jones photograph courtesy of Stockbridge Library Association.)

Employees of the Great Barrington Electric Light Company take a break in North Egremont c. 1910. From left to right are Byron Decker, Clyde Peterson, Harold Lawrence, Edward McCormick, Walter Tuller, Henry Baldwin, Frank Ham, Robert Parrish, and Cy Cooper. (Courtesy of Leveille Collection.)

Hugo Schultes, M.D. (1863–1925) appears ready to make house calls with his fancy new automobile. Dr. Schultes had an office above what is now Tune Street Music on the corner of Main and Railroad Streets in Great Barrington. The good doctor probably didn't have any trouble finding a parking spot in those days. (Courtesy of Richard Hankey.)

Congressman Allen Treadway of Stockbridge campaigns in front of the Red Lion Inn, c. 1920s. No one at the inn objected—since it was owned by Mr. Treadway! (Courtesy of Stockbridge Library Association.)

Could this be Abraham Lincoln stopped at a Great Barrington crosswalk? No, it's Tom McCarty celebrating the town's bicentennial in 1961. Legend has it that he got 50 miles per gallon. (Lucien Aigner photograph courtesy of Great Barrington Historical Society.)

Are two tourists battling for the same parking spot in downtown Stockbridge? No, these airborne antics were actually part of an auto daredevil thrill show at the Great Barrington Fair. (Al Lenardson photograph courtesy of Ice House Studio.)

The Kelloggtown covered bridge in Sheffield collapsed in 1906 when the Reverend Richard Cobden and family of Larchmont, New York, were driving across in a two-horse surrey. All were injured, but amazingly, there were no fatalities. Within days, the bizarre bridge story was picked up by the national news media and greatly embellished. One fictionalized account claimed that the Cobden's baby had floated away in the strong current and was later found downstream—unharmed! Cobden filed a major lawsuit against the town, but that's all water under the bridge now. (Courtesy of Leveille Collection.)

In 1974, the Glendale Middle Road bridge collapsed into the Housatonic River after an unlucky motorist crashed into it. Cuts in state funding delayed the bridge repair for four years. (H.W. Scovill photograph.)

A few feet of snow in Stockbridge isn't going to stop Dewey Beckwith. Git out of the way little doggy. (Courtesy of Stockbridge Library Association.)

All aboard! This hefty train conductor from Van Deusenville gets ready to ride to work on two wheels. (George Soudant photograph courtesy of Jane Anderson Costa.)

34

Great Barrington Police Chief Emmett Shea is ready to pursue bad guys on his super scooter *c*. 1966. (Elmer Lane photograph courtesy of David Lane.)

Great Barrington resident Clarence "Nick" Parrish proudly poses on his Indian Chief motorcycle *c*. 1927. Nick often rode with Harold Finkle, who was the Indian motorcycle dealer in town. (Robert Parrish photograph.)

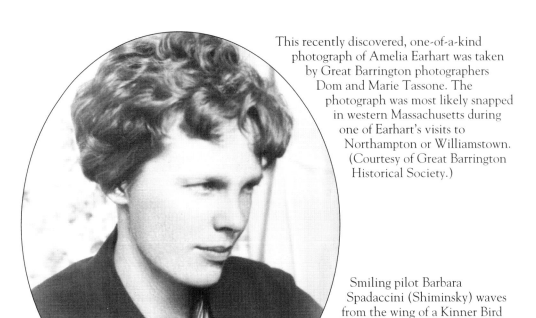

This recently discovered, one-of-a-kind photograph of Amelia Earhart was taken by Great Barrington photographers Dom and Marie Tassone. The photograph was most likely snapped in western Massachusetts during one of Earhart's visits to Northampton or Williamstown. (Courtesy of Great Barrington Historical Society.)

Smiling pilot Barbara Spadaccini (Shiminsky) waves from the wing of a Kinner Bird biplane at the Great Barrington Airport c. 1955. Barbara went on to serve as a flight attendant with two major airlines, and she also worked on a cruise ship line. (Courtesy of Walt Koladza and Berkshire Aviation Enterprises.)

Berkshire aviation pioneers Clarence "Nick" Parrish and Robert "Bob" Parrish operated Parrish Brothers Flying Service. Here they pose with their Brummer-Winkle Bird biplane at the Canaan, Connecticut, airport c. 1931. Bob Parrish later became a captain with American Airlines. (Courtesy of Parrish Collection.)

Future historian, museum curator, and pilot James Parrish is all smiles after his first airplane ride at the Great Barrington Airport in 1953. (Robert Parrish photograph.)

Brothers Louis and John Modolo were early aviation pioneers in Great Barrington. They helped clear the fields for the first landing strip and claimed to be first to land a plane at what is now Great Barrington Airport. Here they pose with their 1927 Waco F plane. (Courtesy of Betsy Holtzinger.)

In 1941, Great Barrington Airport manager Bob Vroom (yes, that was his real last name) and crew grab a wing of his Er Coupe plane. Smiling in the cockpit is Lois Vroom. From left to right are Bob Vroom, Frank Orosz, Walt Koladza, Francis Gargaly, Ed Scholz, George Sebastian, and Sam Howe. (Ted Webster photograph courtesy of Edna Webster Foster.)

Edna Webster Foster of Sheffield began flying in 1937. She often piloted this biplane, owned by Gus Graf, until she gave up the sport in 1938. Edna didn't pilot a plane again until the 1970s, when she again became an accomplished flyer. (Ted Webster photograph.)

This was the scene after West Point Cadet A.J. Horowitz ran out of gas and crashed his training plane into William Graham's home on Cottage Street Extension in Great Barrington. It was May 7, 1945—the day Germany surrendered *and* the day William Graham Jr. returned home from a German prisoner-of-war camp. Remarkably, no one in the house was injured and the pilot escaped with minor injuries. Cadet Horowitz continued flying for the Air Force during the Korean conflict, and then changed his name to James Salter and became a screenwriter and award-winning author. (Courtesy of Leveille Collection.)

Louise (Decker) Koladza and Walt Koladza are ready for take-off in his Er Coupe at the Great Barrington Airport in 1942. (Ted Webster photograph courtesy of Edna Webster Foster.)

This stunning photograph of Louise Koladza was taken in 1946 at the Great Barrington Airport. She was featured in a similar pose on the cover of *Yankee Pilot* magazine the same year. (Ted Webster photograph courtesy of Edna Webster Foster.)

Somebody has to keep those engines running smoothly at the Great Barrington Airport. Rocco Traficante and Donald Moulthrop share the duties in the 1950s. Rocky later became vice president of Berkshire Aviation Enterprises and Don soared sky-high as a captain with Delta Airlines. (Courtesy of Walt Koladza and Berkshire Aviation Enterprises.)

For many years, Great Barrington Airport operated a basement snack bar. In this 1950s view, young Billy Palmer keeps busy waiting on customers. Palmer is now a top administrator at Bradley International Airport in Connecticut. (Courtesy of Walt Koladza and Berkshire Aviation Enterprises.)

Fire trucks are always a favorite in downtown parades. This crowd-pleasing caravan looks sharp as it cruises Great Barrington's Main Street in 1955. The old First National Store looks darn good, too! (Courtesy of Hope Fire Company.)

As the next chapter suggests, you can always go downtown! In the early 1900s, these auto enthusiasts gather in front of the Hotel Miller in Great Barrington. Imagine what would happen if we parked like that today! (Courtesy of Leveille Collection.)

Three
You Can Always
Go Downtown

Norman Rockwell captures the beauty of downtown Stockbridge in one of his most beloved paintings. (Louie Lamone photograph courtesy of Stockbridge Library Association.)

The Red Lion Inn on Main Street in Stockbridge first opened for business about 1778 as Bingham's Tavern. The structure shown here was destroyed by fire in 1896. Just eight months later, *The Berkshire Courier* reported that "A new Red Lion Inn has arisen, phoenix-like, at Stockbridge." Since then, the hotel has become a favorite of Berkshire visitors. Today, the inn is operated with loving care by the Fitzpatrick family and a staff of dedicated employees. (Courtesy of Stockbridge Library Association.)

For nearly seventy years, travelers heading up Prospect Hill from downtown Stockbridge were treated to an impressive sight called Heaton Hall. This grand hotel was built in 1903 by Congressman Allen Treadway, who also owned the Red Lion Inn. By the late 1960s, Heaton Hall had fallen on hard times. Claims of soaring operating costs and maintenance expenses were followed by the razing of the aging structure in 1972. Six years later, affordable housing for senior citizens was constructed on the property. (Courtesy of Leveille Collection.)

It's hard to imagine that the 1864 Jackson Library shown here is part of the same Stockbridge Library structure that exists today. In 1902, the mansard roof and porch were removed. Then, in 1937, a new wing and connecting lobby were added. (Courtesy of Leveille Collection.)

Canadian war heroine Laura Ingersoll Secord was born in this Great Barrington house in 1775. She is honored with several historical markers and statues in Canada and was featured on a postage stamp there in 1992. This Main Street house also served as Great Barrington's free library from 1896 until the present Mason Public Library was built on the site in 1913. (Courtesy of Leveille Collection.)

The Glendale Store, located at the intersection of Route 183 and Glendale Middle Road, also housed the village post office for over one hundred years. In 1963, the store collapsed from the weight of snow on its roof. (Top photograph by David Milton Jones. Both photographs courtesy of Stockbridge Library Association.)

VanDusen's hardware and appliance store was located where the Stockbridge Post Office stands today. A. Wagner, E. Pilling, and M. VanDusen pose during the town's bicentennial celebration in 1939. (Courtesy of Stockbridge Library Association.)

"The Casino" was originally located where the Mission House now stands in Stockbridge (corner of Main and Sergeant Streets). Casino members enjoyed billiards, cards, tennis, a library, and a spacious hall with a fine stage. In 1926, Mabel Choate (daughter of distinguished attorney Joseph Choate) acquired the property. She wanted to clear the lot and move the 1739 home of Reverend John Sergeant (first missionary to the Stockbridge Indians) to the site as a museum. Financier Walter Clark, editor Frank Crowninshield, writer Walter Prichard Eaton, sculptor Daniel Chester French, and Dr. Austen Riggs formed a committee to save the Casino. They purchased property on East Main Street and moved the building to its new home. The Berkshire Playhouse was born! (Lane Brothers photograph.)

Main Street in Stockbridge was home to the Seymour Store in the 1880s. This building was later known as Schilling and Noble Hardware. Today, Williams & Sons Country Store is located here. (Courtesy of Stockbridge Library Association.)

In 1907, Austen Riggs came to Stockbridge to recover from an illness. While recuperating, he studied psychiatry and psychology and later began practicing psychotherapy. Riggs' methods were successful and his practice grew. The Foundation Inn shown here became part of the Riggs Foundation in the 1930s. Today, the Austen Riggs Center continues as an educational facility as well as a world-renowned treatment center for patients who are mentally and emotionally ill. (Courtesy of Leveille Collection.)

The kids in this free-wheeling bike parade roll through downtown Stockbridge in the 1960s or early 1970s. (Clemens Kalischer photograph.)

The Williams Academy/Stockbridge High School on Main Street served local students for many years. By the turn of the twentieth century, this old wooden building had proven inadequate and unsanitary. In 1913, a new Williams High School was constructed directly in front of the old academy building. The impressive, brick structure served as the high school until 1967 when a new regional school was built in Great Barrington. Today, the building is an elementary school. (Courtesy of Leveille Collection.)

The Braman Block in Stockbridge was well-decorated for the town's bicentennial celebration in 1939. From left to right are Jason Braman (who owned Braman's dry goods store), son David Braman, William Sullivan (who had an electrical shop out back), and Manry Jacot (who had a jewelry store here). (Photograph courtesy of David and Anne Braman.)

This was Great Barrington's Main Street c. 1875. On the far left is the Burget & Lewis Block, which housed a hardware store, drugstore, and other businesses. The pillared building next door is the National Mahaiwe Bank. Built in 1847, it was the first bank in town. Both of these buildings were destroyed by fire in 1901 and were replaced by the Mahaiwe Block. The only building in this scene that still survives is the three-story brick structure on the corner of Railroad Street. It is now the T.P. Saddle Blanket Company. This structure was built in 1853 and is the oldest surviving storefront in downtown. (O. Buell photograph courtesy of Great Barrington Historical Commission.)

Hey! Where's Everybody! Main St. Early 1920's

All is quiet in downtown Great Barrington after a snowstorm in the early 1920s. A banner hanging across Main Street reads, "Welcome to Great Barrington, Gateway to the Berkshires." Perhaps it should have read "Brrrkshires!" (Courtesy of Leveille Collection.)

A dapper-looking Earl Jones poses on Great Barrington's Main Street in 1958. At the time he was chairman of a fiscal watchdog group attempting to cut taxes. But he was best known as proprietor of Joneses' Antiques Emporium, which housed an amazing collection of antiques and junktiques that filled four buildings and a field on South Main Street. Guido's Market is on the site today. (William Tague photograph.)

Great Barrington's Railroad Street has always been a busy place. With the arrival of the railroad in 1842, the street was laid out and new buildings erected. A disastrous fire in 1896 wiped out both sides of the street, but it was quickly rebuilt. Once considered a rough part of town, the revitalized street is now lined with trendy shops. (Courtesy of Leveille Collection.)

The Waverly Hotel on Railroad Street in Great Barrington had a poolroom, lunch counter, and a liquor store in 1907. Thriving for a time, the hotel fell on hard times during Prohibition. After a fire in 1928, local police discovered an illegal alcohol still in the basement. The building was later rebuilt and converted into apartments. (R. Lane photograph courtesy of Great Barrington Historical Commission.)

The corner of Main and Castle Streets in Great Barrington looked very different in 1892. A hardware store, drugstore, piano emporium, law office, photography studio, and other businesses were located here. After the buildings burned in 1901, the Mahaiwe Block and Theater were erected on the site. The cannon on the lawn of the town hall was known as "Old Macedonia." It was taken from a British frigate after the War of 1812. During World War II, the cannon was hauled away for scrap. (Lane Brothers photograph courtesy of Great Barrington Historical Society.)

This rare, one-of-a-kind photograph shows Castle Street in Great Barrington just before it was dead-ended by the railroad in 1901. When a new train station was built (a year after this photograph was taken), the railroad tracks were raised, Castle Street was cut off, and a pedestrian subway tunnel was built under the tracks. The Mahaiwe Theater now stands where the wooden building in the right foreground is shown. (Hughes photograph courtesy of Leveille Collection.)

The corner of Main and Bridge Streets in Great Barrington has changed a lot over the years. Easland's Automobile Station was a thriving business in 1910, but the building was later torn down and replaced with an A&P Supermarket. The A&P is shown below in the late 1960s, hiding behind a giant snow bank. This store was later razed and replaced in 1975 with the Pittsfield Cooperative Bank. (Top photograph courtesy of Leveille Collection. Bottom photograph by Elmer Lane.)

Housatonic's Snyder and Race store was a busy place in 1912. People came from all over town to buy groceries, clothing, and hardware. Located on the trolley line at the corner of Main and Pleasant Streets, the building burned in 1923. It was rebuilt and is now known as Jack's Grill. (Fred Sauer photograph courtesy of Froni Crane.)

The Housatonic Grammar School opened in the 1880s. It also housed the high school for a short time. About 1909, it was removed and replaced by the brick elementary school building that still stands today. (Fred Sauer photograph courtesy of Froni Crane.)

In the early 1900s, dirt roads as well as railroads led to the Housatonic train station. With the closing of Monument Mills in the 1950s, the depot's importance to Housatonic greatly diminished. Today, the old station sits quietly on the sidelines, barely noticed in the last-minute rush of a rapidly ending century. (Courtesy of Leveille Collection.)

In 1917, the Great Atlantic and Pacific Tea Company (A&P) operated a store in Housatonic's Shufelt Block. Note the subway sign on the left. (Wonder what the fare was to Grand Central Station?) The store was later known by many names, most recently Ptak's Pleasant Street Market and the Housatonic Country Market. (Fred Sauer photograph courtesy of Great Barrington Historical Society.)

Four

It's a Tough Job, but Somebody's Got to Do It

During the summer months, this small Friendly's in Great Barrington was jam-packed with hungry camp kids, tourists, and locals. The shop opened in 1953, and by 1960 the daily feeding frenzy was handled by, from left to right, Lloyd Sachs, Manager Tom Lawson, Mrs. Fred Oles, Leo Segalla, Randy Bryan, and Carleton Anderson. Friendly's finally moved to larger quarters at its present location on Stockbridge Road in 1965. The building shown here is now the Visiting Nurse Foundation Thrift Shop. (Lucien Aigner photograph courtesy of Great Barrington Historical Society.)

Auctioneer extraordinaire Francis X. MacKoul has a sure-fire way to get people's attention! He gives 'em the gavel! Back in the 1970s, great bargains could often be had at Frank's auctions. In fact, this rare Shaker chair sold for only $10. (Only kidding.) (Marie Tassone photograph courtesy of Great Barrington Historical Society.)

No one could ever call Edward Ely of Great Barrington a lightweight—except when it comes to boxing. Here he is, challenging the photographer to a few rounds c. 1940. Ely battled some formidable foes during his career, including lightweight world champion Willie Pep. You'll have to ask Ed who won! (Courtesy of Ely's Market.)

The late Josephine Ely was longtime proprietor of Ely's Market on State Road in Great Barrington. In her younger days, she worked behind the scenes as a political powerhouse for the Democratic Party. Here we see Senator Ted Kennedy getting good advice while Police Chief William Walsh guards the groceries. (Bernard Drew photograph.)

The Ely family also operated a gas station and auto repair shop next door to their market. Today, this classic Texaco station is barely recognizable—it's decorated with wild colors and is home to Hardcore Sports. (Gladys and John Watson photograph.)

Paul Broverman, Ken Wood, and Frank Szklarz work the counter at Broverman's Market in 1965. Located on State Road in Great Barrington, it was advertised as the store with "everything from a shoestring to a T-Bone." After Broverman's closed, the Pizza House restaurant moved in and has been there ever since. (Courtesy of Mason Public Library.)

Here is the staff of Betros Market in the 1940s. The store is still operated by George Betros at the same Main Street location in Great Barrington. And they said it wouldn't last! (Gladys and John Watson photograph.)

Legend has it that the ever-popular Gorham & Norton's Market in Great Barrington has been on Main Street longer than Main Street! Employees in 1960 include, from left to right, (front row) Charlie Norton, Connie Faxon, Martha Moriarity, Louis Schneider, and Leo Wells; (back row) Tom Sullivan, Murray Tracy, and Walter Burke. (John Watson photograph courtesy of John Tracy.)

Charlie and Roger Schneider confer with Great Barrington oil man Charles Agar and Selectman John Tuller in the 1960s. They're planning a good deed, scout's honor! (Marie Tassone photograph courtesy of Great Barrington Historical Society.)

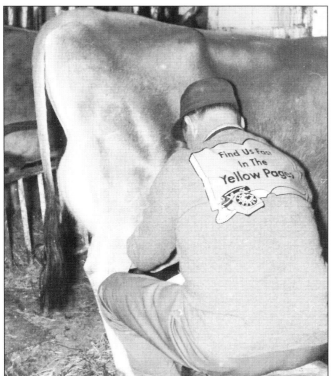

"Hold on, Bessie. I'll have your phone fixed in a few minutes!" Actually, this phone company employee is competing in a cow-milking contest at Jug End resort. Let your fingers do the walking! (Courtesy of Nancy MacDonald Hecker.)

"Hello, sir? What do you mean you're calling from a cow barn?" These Stockbridge telephone operators handled all sorts of strange calls back in the 1950s. (Clemens Kalischer photograph.)

For more than fifty years, the legendary Tom Carey of Stockbridge picked up mail at the train station and carried it to the post office in his horse and buggy. Tourists were often amazed, and then charmed, by the sight of Tom in his old hat and long coat. And speaking of mail, the VanDusen building shown in this 1950s photograph is now the site of—you guessed it—the new Stockbridge Post Office. (William Tague photograph.)

Postal employee Bill Kavanaugh (on right) chats with Great Barrington Postmaster Ray Adams (middle) and mail carrier Paul Larkin in the early 1960s. Coincidentally, Larkin (who left the post office thirty years ago and is self-employed) has been told that he now resembles mailman Clifford Claven from the popular TV sitcom *Cheers*. (Lucien Aigner photograph courtesy of Moulthrop family.)

Florence Markham Boyd delivers the mail in Interlaken with her horse and buggy. She worked for the post office from 1889 until her death in 1947. Interlaken was originally called Curtisville, having been settled by the Curtis family in 1750. At one time, the village bustled with lumber and gristmills, an iron forge, a furniture manufacturer, a machine shop, and the first wood pulp mill in America. (Courtesy of Stockbridge Library Association.)

Electricians John Tracy and Frank Beattie get ready to put up Christmas lights in downtown Great Barrington c. 1930s. (Courtesy of Frank Beattie.)

The Owens brothers began manufacturing paper in Housatonic in the 1850s. By 1873, a clever employee named Henry Cone became proprietor of the firm. He built a huge Victorian factory down river from the old mill but ran out of money before he could install the machinery. The new mill, left abandoned and incomplete, was eventually rescued by businessman Bradley Rising. He took over the defunct factory in 1899 and installed state-of-the-art equipment. Today, Rising Paper employs one hundred and fifty people and uses about one million gallons of calcium-rich, artesian well water each day in the manufacture of high-quality rag papers. (Courtesy of David Rutstein.)

In the 1920s, mountains of rags were examined and cut by hand as the first step in the paper-making process. And you thought your kid's room was messy! (Courtesy of David Rutstein.)

Searles Castle is arguably the most impressive mansion surviving in Great Barrington. Originally called Kellogg Terrace, it was commissioned in 1885 by Mary Frances Hopkins, widow of Central Pacific Railroad tycoon Mark Hopkins (a builder of the first transcontinental railroad). The French Chateau-style mansion was designed by Stanford White, a prominent New York architect. Mrs. Hopkins later married Edward Searles, whom she had hired to supervise the construction and decoration of the mansion. The building is now a private school. (One-of-a-kind photographs by Albert Bodwell courtesy of David Rutstein.)

Mrs. Hopkins' quarry on East Mountain provided the blue dolomite for Searles Castle, as well as for the First Congregational Church. (Bodwell photograph courtesy of David Rutstein.)

This railroad track was built to transport dolomite blocks down the mountainside and across the Housatonic River. (Bodwell photograph courtesy of David Rutstein.)

Huge dolomite blocks were shaped and trimmed at the finishing sheds near Bridge Street, where Memorial Field is today. (Bodwell photograph courtesy of David Rutstein.)

Monument Mills in Housatonic was the largest textile factory in South Berkshire County. The business, which began in 1825, manufactured bedspreads and cotton warp thread. The giant sign atop the cotton storage house was installed in 1915. About 1950, *The Berkshire Courier* reported that Monument Mills "is operating to capacity and the outlook for the future looms very bright." At the time, however, the mill flourished primarily because of military contracts. Once the Korean conflict ended, times got tough. By 1956, the factory had closed, unable to compete against the cheaper labor and lower transportation costs enjoyed by Southern competitors. Today, the remaining mill buildings house a number of cottage industries. (Fred Sauer photograph courtesy of Kinsley Goodrich Collection.)

Marianna Siok was a spooler at Monument Mills in 1939. (James O. Saunders photograph courtesy of Bernard Drew Collection.)

Raymond Moulthrop of Risingdale is all ears after visiting Housatonic barber Fred Sauer in 1957. Moulthrop's grandson, the curious little guy on the left, grew up to be racecar photographer Dave Moulthrop. Sauer was also a talented and prolific photographer. Many of his early 1900s photographs of Housatonic and Stockbridge were sold as prints and postcards. Several appear in this book. (Ruth Moulthrop photograph.)

It's not school we're afraid of, it's the "principal" of the thing! Stockbridge Plain School Principal Dr. Joyce Butler (on right) teams up with teacher Diane Arnold for a Halloween lesson. So when are they going to change into their costumes? (Ann Onymous photograph.)

Mahaiwe Theater Manager Earl Raifstanger, Florence Logan, and Lloyd Height (from left to right) study a secret document in the lobby of the theater. Can't tell you what year it is because the document may still be classified! (Courtesy of Claire and Gordon Height.)

More secret documents! Great Barrington Selectmen Paul White, Lawrence Barbieri, and Cecil "Happy" Brooks (from left to right) study them carefully c. 1950s, but only Happy seems happy about it. (Gladys and John Watson photograph.)

Five

There's No Place Like Home

Mabel Choate proudly poses by the distinctive doorway of her beloved Mission House Museum in Stockbridge c. 1952. Choate was the daughter of noted attorney and American Ambassador to Great Britain Joseph Choate. In 1926, she acquired property on the corner of Sergeant and Main Streets, and moved the 1739 home of Reverend John Sergeant—first missionary to the Stockbridge Indians—to the site, thus creating the Mission House Museum. (William Tague photograph.)

The village of Housatonic. Twenty degrees below zero. Enough said. (Froni Crane photograph.)

This remarkable view of Van Deusenville was painted c. 1859. It depicts the 1833 home of Phineas Chapin, a local farmer and industrialist active in iron smelting and rope manufacture. Note the small railroad train in the right foreground. Monument Mountain towers in the distance. This farmhouse still stands on North Plain Road. (Courtesy of Dale Culleton.)

The Locustwood mansion on Silver Street in Great Barrington was the summer residence of Colonel William Brown, a New York politician and part-owner of the first *New York Daily News*. In 1895, Colonel Brown commissioned the Newsboy fountain that still stands at the intersection of Silver Street and Route 23. Brown also co-founded the Berkshire Trout Hatchery and Wyantenuck Golf Club, and was part-owner of Riverdale Mills on Bridge Street. After Brown's death, his home was turned into a hotel called the Locustwood Inn. An arsonist burned it to the ground in 1931. Today, the crumbling stone framework of Locustwood can still be seen from Silver Street. (Lane Brothers photograph courtesy of Leveille Collection.)

Leo Kaplan was a prominent cattle dealer in Great Barrington. For many years, his happy Holsteins roamed the expansive fields of Merrilea Farms on Silver Street. Fire destroyed a couple of the barns over the years, but most of the remaining structures were flattened by a tornado in 1995. (Marie Tassone photograph courtesy of Great Barrington Historical Society.)

The huge barn on David Leavitt's Brookside estate in Great Barrington was so state-of-the-art that Horace Greeley visited the place in 1855. He was greatly impressed and wrote of his visit for the *New York Tribune*. Leavitt, a banker and president of the Housatonic Railroad, built the huge structure into a hillside. It had three entrance levels, plus a brook running through the building that powered saw and gristmills. The barn burned to the ground in 1885. (Courtesy of Leveille Collection.)

The Brookside estate's library and music room, shown here *c.* 1914, was itself a work of art. Electrical engineer William Stanley purchased Brookside from railroad tycoon David Leavitt. The main building burned in 1904 and was being rebuilt by Stanley when he lost a major lawsuit to corporate giant Westinghouse Electric. Driven out of business, Stanley sold Brookside in 1907 to Eastman Kodak executive William H. Walker. In the 1940s and 50s, Brookside was a private school. It is now the Eisner Camp for Living Judaism. (Edwin Hale Lincoln photograph courtesy of Leveille Collection.)

William H. Walker, Eastman Kodak business executive, inventor, and the "Baron of Brookside," sent this "urn-est" portrait of himself as part of his 1914 Christmas greetings. (Courtesy of Leveille Collection.)

Italian landscape architects and a multitude of assistants created gorgeous gardens at the Brookside estate in Great Barrington. Statues of gods, goddesses, and children were showcased among marble pillars and an astounding array of exotic plantings. Ornate walls and fancy gates featured the faces of gargoyles, monks, and supposedly, the stone masons who worked on the property. (Edwin Hale Lincoln photograph courtesy of Leveille Collection.)

Great Barrington's William Stanley was an electrical engineering genius. More than one hundred and twenty patents were issued in his name, including many for products that revolutionized the distribution of electricity. Mr. Stanley was the first to develop a practical system for transmitting alternating electrical current over long distances. In short, he made it economical and safe to bring electricity into homes and businesses. One of his other inventions was the Stanley insulated vacuum bottle. (Courtesy of Wyantenuck Country Club.)

In 1907, William Stanley sold his magnificent estate on Brookside Road in Great Barrington and moved to this smaller, but still elegant, home on Maple Avenue. He called his house Chestnutwood, and it was here that he died in 1916. In 1957, the house was converted into a nursing home. A larger facility was eventually needed and the residence was razed after the current brick facility was built. (Courtesy of Leveille Collection.)

In the early 1700s, the Stockbridge Mahican Indians came under the protective eye of missionary, minister, and friend John Sargeant. Prospects brightened for the local Native Americans until Sargeant's death in 1749. Before long, they were coerced into leaving and headed to the West. More than a century later, Mary Hopkins Goodrich, great-granddaughter of Sergeant and founder of the Laurel Hill Association, erected this memorial at the site of the ancient Indian burial ground. (Courtesy of Stockbridge Library Association.)

Mahican Indians and friends celebrate their return to Stockbridge and Great Barrington during the nation's bicentennial in 1976. (Al Lenardson photograph courtesy of Ice House Studio.)

Look carefully and you'll see two brave tree trimmers in the branches of the diseased elm tree. The tree toppling took place in the 1930s next to a building originally known as The Inn at Curtisville (now Interlaken). This stately hotel was built in 1834 and also housed a tavern as well as a store. In 1892, John and Helen Parsons purchased the inn and turned it into a fresh-air retreat called St. Helen's Home. Until 1931, the home provided a healthy summertime experience for needy New York City children. Today the building is a private residence. (David Milton Jones photograph courtesy of Stockbridge Library Association.)

Naumkeag, summer home of Ambassador Joseph H. Choate, was designed by renowned architect Stanford White in 1886. The surrounding gardens were the inspiration of daughter Mabel Choate. Members of the Choate family summered at Naumkeag from 1887 until 1958. Upon her death, Mabel Choate bequeathed the house and its contents to the Trustees of Reservations. (Courtesy of Judy Rupinski.)

A giant boulder off Alford Road in Great Barrington was a favorite meeting place of neighborhood children in the 1920s. They called it Simon's Rock. The original cabin at Simon's Rock was begun in 1924 by fourteen-year-old Elizabeth Blodgett (Hall) and her friends. Mrs. Hall went on to a distinguished academic career and founded Simon's Rock College in 1964. (Courtesy of Simon's Rock College of Bard.)

If you feel like going fishing, Mr. Sackett of Sackett's Boat House on Stockbridge Bowl will probably rent you a rowboat. Don't suppose he accepts credit cards, though. (Courtesy of Leveille Collection.)

Whatever happened to Angelo's Snack Bar on Stockbridge Road in Great Barrington? It became Bill Whittaker's new home in the late 1960s! Thirty years later, Whittaker still dabbles in auto sales just down the street. Ask and he'll probably throw in a copy of this book with every car you buy. (Elmer Lane photograph.)

Located on Route 7 near Monument Mountain Reservation, Squaw Peak Tourist Camp was a scenic stopover for Berkshire visitors. The cabins, campground, snack bar, souvenir stand, and gas station were owned by the Ed Damms family until the early 1950s. The Briarcliff Motor Lodge was built just north of the site in 1961. (Fred Sauer photograph courtesy of Great Barrington Historical Society.)

Stockbridge sculptor Daniel Chester French (1850–1931) was a man of many talents. Over the years, he transformed his old Glendale farm into the gorgeous estate he called Chesterwood. He personally created and cared for the gardens adjoining his studio, shown here. A handcar on railroad tracks enabled the sculptor and his assistants to roll a work in progress from the studio out into full sunlight. (Steven Arnold photograph.)

A guardian angel watches over this relaxed visitor at Chesterwood in the 1950s. The gentleman is not identified, but a notation on the back of the photograph indicates that Mr. French's daughter, Margaret French Cresson, ordered one copy of the print. (Marie Tassone photograph courtesy of Great Barrington Historical Society.)

This Spanish-style mansion was originally known as Stonyhurst. Owned by wealthy summer resident C.L. Wetherbee, it was located near the intersection of Route 23 and 71 in Great Barrington. The estate later served as a popular hotel. In the 1950s and '60s, the property was part of a private school known as Cornwall Academy. Fire destroyed the building in 1971, and a private housing development now occupies the site. (Courtesy of Leveille Collection.)

During the summer of 1887, William E. Tefft, a wholesaler from New York City, visited Great Barrington. He liked the area so much that he cleared a lot across from the fairground and built this Victorian mansion. After Tefft died, his home became a prep school known as Hallock School. In 1947, the school made headlines when it was purchased by the Moorish Science Temple, an African-American religious sect. In 1963, the house was torn down and a shopping center was built on the site (now Big Y and Ames). (Courtesy of Leveille Collection.)

South Main Street in Great Barrington has long been an expansive thoroughfare, as shown in this 1892 view. Wainwright Hall, on the left, was built in 1766 and completely remodeled by owner Franklin Pope in 1890. Pope was a well-known artist, editor, engineer, and inventor who worked briefly in partnership with Thomas Edison. Pope also helped develop breakthrough electrical technology working with inventor William Stanley. Wainwright Hall is now a charming bed and breakfast inn. (Lane Brothers photograph courtesy of Jim Kotleski.)

In the late 1800s, hermit George Crosby's shack was as famous as any Berkshire estate. It was located in Great Barrington near the gorge between Grove and Bentley Streets. Legend has it that as a young man, Crosby fell in love with Alice Skermerhorn, but she apparently jilted him for another. His heart broken, Crosby became reclusive and eccentric, but continued to operate a small ferryboat (which he named *Alice*) on the Housatonic River. In 1891, he was examined by doctors and sent to a Northampton asylum. Crosby's few personal effects were auctioned off, and among them was a faded photograph of his beloved Alice. (Lane Brothers photograph courtesy of Jim Kotleski.)

The Oakwood Inn was a popular summer hotel located off Taconic Avenue in Great Barrington. It was built as a residence for Edward Brainard, a wealthy businessman who helped develop this part of town. The house was later converted into a seasonal hotel and greatly enlarged. In 1975, the aging Oakwood Inn was torn down. Nine years later, upscale condominiums were built on the site. (Courtesy of Leveille Collection.)

The Sedgwick Institute was established in 1841 by James Sedgwick, a Williams College graduate. Operated by the Van Lennep family for many years, the Great Barrington prep school had an excellent reputation. Although the Sedgwick school building shown here may not look familiar, it still stands north of Ward's Garden Center on South Main Street. In the 1930s, the first floor was removed and the building was converted into a residence (and later a church). It is now Kleinwald's Antiques. (Lane Brothers photograph courtesy of Jim Kotleski.)

Six

Hands to Work,
Hearts to God

These angelic youngsters are preparing for First Communion at the Corpus Christi Catholic Church in Housatonic in the late 1950s. (Tassone photograph courtesy of Great Barrington Historical Society.)

These young ladies are ready to march at Belcher Square in Great Barrington. All Saints' Catholic church has been an active participant in local parades for many years. (Elmer Lane photograph.)

Worshippers pose with the Reverend Joseph Forte at the Macedonia Baptist Church on Rosseter Street in Great Barrington. The congregation was founded in 1944 by Isaac and Martha Crawford. (Leveille photograph.)

Ahavath Sholom Synagogue on North Street in Great Barrington was chartered in 1926 as Love of Peace Synagogue. Rabbi Jacob Axelrod began his service the same year. He also operated a small delicatessen next door to the synagogue, shown here in 1980. (Donald B. Victor photograph.)

Rabbi Deborah Zecher of Hevrah of Southern Berkshire welcomes students to the Torah for Tots program. The synagogue celebrates its twentieth anniversary in 1997. (Courtesy of Hevrah of Southern Berkshire.)

Eden Hill Chapel and Monastery at Marian Fathers in Stockbridge is visited by thousands of people each year. (Elmer Lane photograph.)

St. Paul's Episcopal Church in Stockbridge has a beautiful baptistery, as shown in this 1892 view. (Lane Brothers photograph.)

St. Joseph's Catholic Church is an often-photographed sanctuary located on Elm Street in Stockbridge. (William Uhler photograph courtesy of Stockbridge Library Association.)

The First Church of Christ Scientist in Great Barrington, shown here c. 1940s, was originally the home of noted doctor C.T. Collins. (Ted Webster photograph.)

The Methodist Church in Great Barrington is one of the oldest church structures in town. (John Taylor photograph.)

St. James' Episcopal Church in Great Barrington still had its old parsonage next door in 1890. (Lane Brothers photograph.)

A Rudolf Steiner School student is all smiles as she cleans up debris along Great Barrington's River Walk. The winding walkway remains a work in progress and is the vision of project coordinator Rachel Fletcher. In the early 1980s, the River Walk began as a one-time effort to clean up trash behind a riverfront building. Each year, hundreds of volunteers continue their labor of love by extending the nature trail farther along the river. (Rachel Fletcher photograph.)

The River Walk bucket brigade makes the job easier for all. (Rachel Fletcher photograph.)

Hannah Kirchner digs in at a 1992
River Walk work session. (Rachel
Fletcher photograph.)

Trail designer Peter Jensen battles a boulder with Tony Manzon. The rock lost. (Rachel
Fletcher photograph.)

The Children's Chime Tower was given to Stockbridge in 1878 by noted attorney David Dudley Field as a memorial to his children and grandchildren. (Field's brother Cyrus built the first transatlantic telegraph cable.) The tower marks the spot where missionary John Sergeant preached to the Stockbridge Indians in 1739. According to Field's wishes, the chimes are rung every evening from "apple blossom time until frost." (Courtesy of Stockbridge Library Association.)

Alva Ernest Gray played the chimes in the tower from 1929 until his retirement in 1975. The tower holds ten bells, most weighing 8,000 pounds. (Clemens Kalischer photograph.)

Easter celebrants gather for a service at the Laurel Hill Grove in Stockbridge c. 1950. The Laurel Hill Association was founded in 1853 as the first village-improvement organization in the United States. Today, the association continues to preserve and protect the natural beauty of Stockbridge. (Clemens Kalischer photograph.)

Members of the Stockbridge Congregational Church get ready to flip their wigs during the church's bicentennial celebration in 1934. This ecstatic crowd includes, from left to right, (front row) Mrs. J. Schilling, Betty Truran, George Seeley, the Reverend C. Fisher, Mrs. Fisher, and Mrs. F. Sedgell; (back row) Fannie Wells, Edmund Wilcox, Mrs. C. Watkins, Mrs. F. Seeley, Leroy Smith, Anna Luffburrow, Jane Seymour, and George Warner. (Courtesy of Stockbridge Library Association.)

In 1910, Mary Mason, a summer resident of Great Barrington, bequeathed a sizable sum and property for the founding of a hospital. Unfortunately, her will was contested and the eventual compromise resulted in less-than-adequate funding. Despite this setback, Fairview Hospital was formed in 1912 and was housed in this clapboard building. It still stands on West Avenue. (Courtesy of Leveille Collection.)

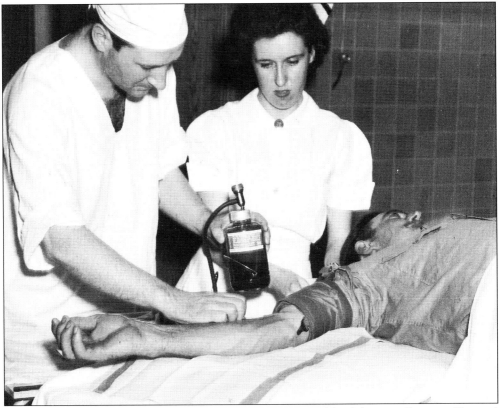

Dr. Arthur Cassel and Nurse Ann (Tully) Walsh stick it to a blood donor at Fairview Hospital in 1942. (Photograph courtesy of Ann Walsh. Blood donation courtesy of Sheldon Fenn.)

The magnificent Roosevelt organ can still be heard and enjoyed at the First Congregational Church in Great Barrington. The organ has nearly four thousand pipes and cost $40,000 in 1883. (A bargain at $10 per pipe!) It was the gift of Timothy Hopkins, son of railroad tycoon Mark Hopkins (and descendant of the first minister). (Courtesy of Leveille Collection.)

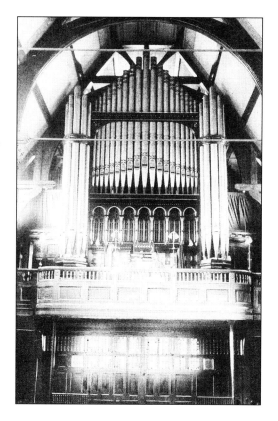

The first St. Peter's Church in Great Barrington was built in 1854 on the corner of Cottage and Russell Streets, now the site of St. Peter's Center. Construction of the present St. Peter's Church on Main Street began in 1904, using huge marble blocks mined from an Egremont quarry. (W.H. Van Patten photograph courtesy of Great Barrington Historical Society.)

Agnes Goodyear Gould was the co-founder of Gould Farm, a residential rehabilitation community in Monterey for people with mental illness. After the death of her husband Will Gould in 1925, Agnes assumed the leadership of the farm. She died in 1958. Today, Gould Farm is a highly respected recuperation center offering a healing milieu of care, work, rest, and counseling. (Lucien Aigner photograph courtesy of Gould Farm.)

The Reverend Jean Morgan of the First Congregational Church in Great Barrington and Rabbi Jacob Axelrod of Ahavath Sholom Synagogue compare biblical quotations during a 1983 interfaith meeting. In the background, the Reverend Joseph Forte of the Macedonia Baptist Church confers with an associate. (Donald B. Victor photograph.)

The Berkshire Symphonic Festival, predecessor of Tanglewood, was born in 1934 when noted conductor/composer Henry Hadley offered to give concerts in the Berkshires "under the stars." That summer, the New York Philharmonic Orchestra performed on the edge of the horse show ring at the Hanna Farm in Interlaken (now the DeSisto School). (David Milton Jones photograph courtesy of Stockbridge Library Association.)

The line forms here for tickets to the first Berkshire Symphonic Festival concert held in 1934. Three thousand people attended. Two years later, Dr. Serge Koussevitzky of the Boston Symphony Orchestra was hired. In 1937, festival concerts were held in a tent on an estate now known by millions of music lovers as Tanglewood. (David Milton Jones photograph courtesy of Stockbridge Library Association.)

It will be months before Aaron Copeland's "Appalachian Spring" springs forth from the Tanglewood shed. In the meantime, the sweet dripping of maple sap is music to the ears of this syrup maker, c. 1960. (William Tague photograph.)

A row of sheet music leads to the master at work! Leonard Bernstein enjoys teaching talented students at Tanglewood in 1987. (Walter H. Scott photograph.)

The Fraternity of Ancient Free and Accepted Masons is the oldest and largest fellowship organization in the world. The charter of the Mason's Cincinnatus Lodge in Great Barrington was signed by patriot (and Mason Grand Master) Paul Revere in 1795. As part of the local lodge's centennial celebration in 1895, their hall, located in the Berkshire House (at the corner of Main and Bridge Streets), was decorated with banners and a giant portrait of George Washington. (Costello photograph courtesy of Great Barrington Historical Commission.)

Members of Great Barrington's Hope Fire Company pose in front of the Berkshire House hotel in 1874. Several in the group are carrying musical instruments and the rest of the gang guards the 1854 pumper and hose cart. Ironically, the Berkshire House burned down in 1901. (Courtesy of Leveille Collection.)

What a blast! In 1953, the women's auxiliary of the Glendale Fire Department receives instructions from District Fire Warden Francis Mahoney on how to fight forest fires. From left to right are Mahoney, Gladys Burroughs, Frances Antoniazzi, Dorothea Miller, Margaret Schneyer, Helen Miller, and Corinne Cooper. (Courtesy of Glendale Hose Company No 3.)

Stockbridge Hose Company No. 1 was established in 1894 and a fire station was built on Elm Street two years later. Proud members of the fire department pose outside the station in 1931. (Courtesy of Francis Pilling.)

Members of Great Barrington's Hope Fire Company gather in front of Firemen's Hall on Bridge Street *c.* 1895. The station stood near the current site of Laramee's Cleaners. (Courtesy of Hope Fire Company.)

The Glendale Fire Department was organized in 1905. This view was taken a few years later. (Fred Sauer photograph courtesy of Frank Ptak.)

Firemen fight the flames at Great Barrington's popular Melvin's Pharmacy in 1978. One can't help but see the irony of the sign that exclaims "Home Cooking!" (Photograph courtesy of Hope Fire Company.)

With hands to work and hearts to God, these two workers stand proudly next to their recently completed steeple, high atop the Corpus Christi Catholic Church in Housatonic, c. 1911. (Fred Sauer photograph courtesy of Frank Ptak.)

Seven
Beauty or the Beast

Three sisters wonder what to do next as their friend enjoys a snack at the Stockbridge Harvest Festival. Held as a fundraiser for the Berkshire Botanical Garden since the mid-1930s, the festival is a favorite of locals and tourists alike. (Clemens Kalischer photograph.)

A smiling threesome happily hold hands at a South County music festival in 1990. (David Wade Smith photograph.)

Have you ever heard the story of *Little Two-headed Riding Hood?* She lives in Great Barrington, not too far from Grandma's house. You should see what Grandma looks like! (Steven Arnold photograph.)

A prize-winning pumpkin poses with a very excited young lady at the Great Barrington Fair. You can't get much cuter than this! (Marie Tassone photograph courtesy of Great Barrington Historical Society.)

This "cat-ankerous" kitty has hissy-fits with her canine companion every summer day. Located at the intersection of Main and South Streets in Stockbridge, the Cat and Dog Fountain has delighted passersby for over one hundred and thirty years. Harsh New England weather eventually corroded the original statue, so a sculpted replica was installed in 1976. (Courtesy of Stockbridge Library Association.)

Clarence "Nick" Parrish was a lineman for New England Telephone when this diamondback rattlesnake attacked his boot on Great Barrington's East Mountain *c.* 1926. It looks like Nick's boot won. (Robert Parrish photograph.)

Summer campers at the Brookside School in Great Barrington prepare to rob the rich to pay the poor in their version of *Robin Hood*. No one in this photograph is identified, but it was probably taken in the 1940s. (Marie Tassone photograph courtesy of Great Barrington Historical Society.)

Tuesday Weld is the beauty *and* the beast in the 1968 movie *Pretty Poison*. Filmed in Great Barrington and North Egremont in 1967, the cult classic stars Tony Perkins as a naive parolee who falls in love with a beautiful, but insanely manipulative, young woman (Weld). The psychological thriller was based on Stephen Geller's first novel, *She Let Him Continue*. (Movie Star News photograph courtesy of Bernard Drew Collection.)

The tall guy in this picture welcomes youngsters to the Stockbridge Harvest Festival in the 1940s. The big lug doesn't talk much, but the kids say he does a great job of scaring the crows away. (Courtesy of Berkshire Botanical Garden.)

These guys look proud as peacocks at the Great Barrington Fair. Apparently their chicken won first place in the egg-laying contest. Unfortunately, the losers cried fowl and the judges flew the coop. (Marie Tassone photograph courtesy of Great Barrington Historical Society. Humor courtesy of Great Barrington Hysterical Society.)

Ethel Parrish (Kotarba) guards her fine-feathered hen friends on the back porch of her Silver Street home in Great Barrington. Perhaps Colonel Sanders was in the neighborhood and she didn't want to take any chances. (Robert Parrish photograph.)

The road to Beartown State Forest never looked more beautiful than it did during the winter of 1965. (Walter H. Scott photograph.)

The Devil's Pulpit atop Monument Mountain is considered by some to be misnamed. With such a magnificent view, perhaps God's Pulpit or Mother Nature's Pulpit would be more appropriate. (Arthur Palme photograph courtesy of Stockbridge Library Association.)

The Berkshire Inn stood proudly on Great Barrington's Main Street where Bill's Pharmacy and the Berkshire Motor Inn are today. Built in 1893, the inn was considered one of the most impressive structures in all of South Berkshire County. This idealized version of the inn was painted *c.* 1900. After a third-floor fire in 1965, the hotel was torn down. Many longtime residents wish the structure had been saved and still mourn the loss. (Courtesy of Judy Rupinski.)

Left: Determined firefighters aim at the flames during the Berkshire Inn fire of 1965. (Elmer Lane photograph.)

Right: The last of the fire is knocked down where an older section of the inn connected to a newer addition. Luckily, the old outer wall was still intact under the roof, forming a block in the attic that slowed the fire's progress. (Elmer Lane photograph.)

For more than fifty years, Tom Carey of Stockbridge picked up mail at the train station and carried it to the post office in his horse and buggy. He and his horse were a familiar site in downtown Stockbridge well into the 1950s. (Clemens Kalischer photograph.)

The de Lancey Memorial may be one of the best-kept secrets in Great Barrington. Located out of view in the Mahaiwe Cemetery, these "angels among us" usually escape the attention of passersby. Children in particular enjoy climbing up onto the massive marble bench and "talking" to the angels. Local artist Darragh de Lancey created the sculpture in 1926–27 as a memorial to his daughter Harriet, who died unexpectedly while attending Smith College. (Leveille photograph.)

New York banker-philanthropist Anson Phelpes Stokes owned this 100-room "cottage" on a hill overlooking Stockbridge Bowl. Beginning in 1892, Mrs. Stokes supervised the building of the mansion on property named "Shadow Brook" years earlier by writer Nathaniel Hawthorne. Shadowbrook was later purchased by Andrew Carnegie because it reminded him of his native Scotland and because he enjoyed fishing at Stockbridge Bowl. Shadowbrook became a Jesuit monastery in 1922. (Courtesy of Leveille Collection.)

In March 1956, one of the most tragic fires in Berkshire County history destroyed the Shadowbrook Novitiate on Route 183 in Stockbridge. Four Jesuits were killed and six other priests and brothers were injured. The following year, a new brick building was erected on the site. By the early 1970s, few students were training to become Jesuit priests and the seminary was closed. In 1981, Shadowbrook was purchased by the Kripalu Center, a holistic health and yoga retreat. (Gene Mitchell photograph courtesy of Stockbridge Fire Department.)

Eldon's Cave was discovered in 1875 by fourteen-year-old Eldon French. It is located near Great Barrington on what is now private property. Considered the second-longest cave in New England, it was a popular spelunking site for many years. Now, because of safety concerns and an increasingly litigious society, the cave's location is kept secret. Special permission to photograph the entrance was granted to the author and his associates.

Donald Paisley crawls through Eldon's Cave in 1941. The narrow limestone walls feature colorful bands of blue, yellow, green, and orange. The cave also has a miniature waterfall and a tiny pond. (Arthur Palme photograph courtesy of Berkshire Country Historical Society.)

Is this a "Star Trek" crewmember aiming her phasor at a cave-dwelling Horta? No, it's actually a brave Berkshire spelunker shining her flashlight on a stalactite in Egremont's Crystal Cave c. 1940. (Arthur Palme photograph courtesy of Berkshire County Historical Society.)

"Honey, I shrunk Bash Bish Falls!" Spelunker Roger Johnson discovers a miniature waterfall in an Egremont cave c. 1940. (Arthur Palme photograph courtesy of Berkshire County Historical Society.)

The Housatonic River misbehaves as it spills its banks onto Park Street in Stockbridge c. 1936. Wonder if MacClintic's Garage will be selling ice instead of gasoline? (David Milton Jones photograph courtesy of Stockbridge Library Association.)

The Memorial Day tornado of 1995 ripped through portions of Egremont, Great Barrington, and Monterey, leaving a path of death and destruction. (Leveille photograph.)

Eight

Family, Friends, and Neighbors

The Mahaiwe Theater marquee says it all. This clever photo was taken in 1982, before Great Barrington Police Officer William Walsh became police chief. (Donald B. Victor photograph.)

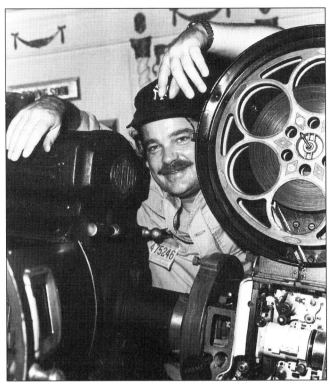

Former Mahaiwe Theater manager Al Schwartz poses with the old Brenkert-Simplex projection system that was replaced in the 1980s. (Donald B. Victor photograph courtesy of Bernard Drew.)

Future movie stars await discovery while watching Great Barrington's 1993 Hometown Heroes Parade. (Leveille photograph.)

A Stockbridge Town Meeting in the 1950s is reminiscent of a Norman Rockwell painting. Or, is it the other way around? (Clemens Kalischer photograph.)

Beloved teacher and former Stockbridge Selectman Mary Flynn enjoys a summer day with retired Tanglewood Manager Todd Perry. (Clemens Kalischer photograph.)

Laurie McLeod is an award-winning, independent choreographer based in Stockbridge. Her contemporary dance theater work is well known for its quirky humor and visual imagery. McLeod has performed throughout the world, and her dance troupe recently traveled above the Arctic Circle to perform for two remote mining communities. She also produces dance movement videos for children. (Sanjiban Sellow photograph.)

For over twenty years, Olga Dunn has been training dancers, producing original choreography, and presenting performances throughout the Northeast. Her affiliated school specializes in classical ballet, modern, and jazz styles. This photograph of Dunn by Lindy Smith was originally printed in platinum, in a process rarely used today because it is so expensive. Platinum prints possess a tonal quality that often gives them an almost three-dimensional look. (Courtesy of Lindy Smith.)

On Thanksgiving weekend in 1965, Stockbridge Police Chief William Obanhein arrested young Arlo Guthrie for improperly disposing of garbage. Guthrie later embellished the event in his classic song, "Alice's Restaurant Massacree." In 1969, the legendary saga was made into a motion picture. Chief Obanhein, better known as "Officer Obie," played himself in the film. Guthrie and Obanhein became friends while making the movie and later teamed up as judges at a local bartending contest. (Edgar Zukauskas photograph courtesy of Ice House Studio.)

During the autumn of 1996, Arlo Guthrie re-recorded "Alice's Restaurant Massacree," adding a few new lyrics. The fundraising event was performed before a live audience and broadcast on nationwide radio on Thanksgiving Day. (Kelly Gray photograph.)

Richard Nixon joins four brothers for pizza—at Four Brothers Pizza Inn! Kris, George, Peter, and John Stefanopoulos own the restaurant in Great Barrington as well as several in New York state. This view was taken in front of their Hillsdale, New York, eatery. (Marie Tassone photograph courtesy of Great Barrington Historical Society.)

While Nixon enjoys his pizza, it appears that Ted and Joan Kennedy prefer barbecued ribs prepared by Butternut Basin owner Channing Murdock. (Marie Tassone photograph courtesy of Great Barrington Historical Society.)

Fallen comrades are remembered on Memorial Day in front of the Great Barrington Town Hall in the 1960s. (Marie Tassone photograph courtesy of Great Barrington Historical Society.)

World War I soldiers, children, and residents march through the Stockbridge town cemetery. (Courtesy of Stockbridge Library Association.)

Civil rights leader, author, educator, and visionary W.E.B. DuBois (1868–1963) was born and raised in Great Barrington. He grew up in a small farmhouse, no longer standing, on Route 23 near South Egremont. A memorial plaque was installed at his birth site on Church Street in 1994. Guest speaker at the ceremony was David Levering Lewis, winner of the Pulitzer Prize for the first volume in his DuBois biography. (Photograph courtesy of Mason Public Library.)

Stockbridge resident David Gunn poses with a portrait of his famous ancestor, Agrippa Hull (1759–1848). Their likeness in this 1973 photograph is startling. The portrait, on display in the Stockbridge Library, was painted from an 1840s daguerreotype. Agrippa Hull served in the American Revolution as an aide to Colonel John Paterson of Lenox and to Polish General Thadeusz Kosciuszko. After six years in the Continental Army, Hull worked for Congressman Theodore Sedgwick in Stockbridge and Washington. (Courtesy of Stockbridge Library Association.)

Sculptor Daniel Chester French is perhaps best known for creating the seated *Abraham Lincoln* (1922) for the Lincoln Memorial in Washington. French did much of the work on the Lincoln at Chesterwood, and smaller versions of the sculpture are still in his Glendale studio. (Courtesy of Chesterwood, a National Trust Historic Site.)

Photojournalist Lucien Aigner pioneered the use of the 35mm "miniature" candid camera. Many of his dramatic photographs in the 1930s reflected a European continent drifting toward war. Aigner's portrait subjects ranged from Winston Churchill to Benito Mussolini to Albert Einstein. He came to the United States in 1936 and snapped fascinating views of New York City, and Harlem in particular. Aigner moved to Great Barrington in 1954 and opened a studio here. He celebrates his 96th birthday in September 1997. This photograph of Aigner by Lindy Smith was originally printed in platinum. (Courtesy of Lindy Smith.)

Veteran radio newsman Tom Jaworski of Great Barrington hams it up with his ham radio in this 1960s view. According to Jaworski, he has been broadcasting at WSBS radio "since Marconi was a pup." (Marie Tassone photograph courtesy of Great Barrington Historical Society.)

These three guys have revolutionized television viewing in these parts! Community Television for the Southern Berkshires (CTSB) presents an interesting array of programming produced primarily by volunteers. But the station is best known for broadcasting local selectmen's meetings in Sheffield, Great Barrington, Stockbridge, Lee, and Lenox. These often-controversial meetings have boosted community involvement in local politics. From left to right are CTSB executive director Shawn Serre, production coordinator David Cachat, and operations manager Dan Miller. (Leveille photograph.)

Anne Braman of Stockbridge posed as the schoolteacher for Norman Rockwell's 1956 painting *Happy Birthday, Miss Jones*. The painting appeared on the cover of the *Saturday Evening Post*. Here she speaks to a group at the Red Lion Inn about the experience. (Donald B. Victor photograph.)

At Jug End resort in Egremont, Olympic ski champion Penny Pitou and Nancy-Fay MacDonald get ready for the winter of 1961. (Courtesy of Nancy MacDonald Hecker.)

Norman Rockwell and carpenter/cabinetmaker Ejner Handberg admire Rockwell's new studio shortly after Handberg finished building it in 1957. (W.H. Scovill photograph courtesy of Stockbridge Library Association.)

Stockbridge historian Polly Pierce and Molly Rockwell share a smile in 1970. She who laughs, lasts! (Courtesy of Stockbridge Library Association.)